Change Becomes Us

Amy Laurens

OTHER WORKS

SANCTUARY SERIES
Where Shadows Rise
Through Roads Between
When Worlds Collide

KADITEOS SERIES
How Not To Acquire A
    Castle

**STORM FOXES
SERIES**
A Fox Of Storms And
    Starlight
A Stag Of Snow And
    Memory

SHORTER WORKS
Bones Of The Sea
Dreaming of Forests
Rush Job
Trust Issues

COLLECTIONS
April Showers
Darkness And Good

It All Changes Now
Of Sea Foam And Blood
The Inklet Collection

POETRY & PLAYS
Change Becomes Us
For A Little While
Where Your Treasure Is

NON-FICTION
How To Write Dogs
How To Theme
How To Create Cultures
How To Create Life
How To Map
How To Plan A Pinterest-
    Worthy Party Without Dying
On The Origin Of
    Paranormal Species
The 32 Worst Mistakes
    People Make About Dogs

Find other works by the author:
www.AmyLaurens.com

CHANGE BECOMES US

AMY LAURENS

AUSTRALIA

Print ISBN: 978-1-922434-51-7
eBook ISBN: 9798215990322

www.inkprintpress.com

National Library of Australia Cataloguing-in-Publication Data
Laurens, Amy 1985—
Change Becomes Us
118 p.   cm.
ISBN: 978-1-922434-51-7
Inkprint Press, Canberra, Australia
1. Poetry—Women Authors 2. Poetry—Australian & Oceanian
3. Poetry—Subjects & Themes—Death, Grief, Loss 4. Poetry—
Subjects & Themes—Inspirational & Religious

Summary: Poetry about grieving for the old and making space for the new in a season of life change.

First Edition: March 2023

Cover design © Inkprint Press.
Cover image © Milan Popovic via Unsplash

CONTENTS

A TEACHER'S FALL

Your face never
belonged to me.
I was loaned it
for a while, by
due process and
bureaucratic regard,
never once suspecting
I'd come to regard
it as one of my own.

I fall in love every year.
And it is a fall:
A great gust of wind
sweeping pretence away,
stripping leaves that,
golden though they be,
do little aught but hide
the beauty of the trunk beneath.

It takes five weeks to fall.

And at the end of each year,
I am left, stripped bare and bereft,
a tree removed from a forest
or a forest removed of its trees
breathing air that was intended
to be shared by many sets of lungs.

Winter, summer, spring and fall,
only the annual dance is this:
—a falling—
—a glorious summer of ponder-ful delight—
—then winter, cold and bare.
You do not need me anymore,
and this is right.

One day, my heart will find a spring,
and heal from this annual decay.

ART IS LIGHT

Art is light
when all is dark
reminding us that something greater spins
around the pivotal gaps in our understanding
around the Swiss-cheese holes in our hearts

When the night is black and the world is grey
When the night is deep and the world is shallow
When the press hounds bay and corporate wolves nip
When the sadness stains your soul like oil,
and your soul is a sponge, poisoned
fetid and rank because of what was allowed to grow
there
know this:

It's art to which we turn.
Abstract colours refracting the vibrations of the
  universe
Wriggling air that tugs at the strings of the spirit
Black dots on pages white, encoding nothing
more or less
than the very soul of what it means to human...

Art is light
The world is a riot
Let us throw the torch.

ART IS DARK

Art is dark
when all is light
a soft, warm gentleness that eases
bright, harsh spotlights from our eyes
to sooth away the sharpness of the world
pointed pens like lances
sharpened tongues like daggers
DMs turned DOA
newsprint turned newspaste
floodlights brimming over, spilling
into the very corners of our souls
leaving no intimate pebble unscoured.

Art is a mushroom, gently unfolding,
skirts drawn close, fragile and lacy,
caps riotous and red or else purple and moist
gleaming green and burnished brown
egg-white and charcoal black
that fungal god of decay that, ever-present,
reminds us of our own fragility
as something to gently nourish
and protect.

Art is the soft dimming of a callous voice
a calming, insistent call to peace
or else to war against the light that scourges
every shadow from the land
every place of refuge
casting all into sharp relief, demanding
this or that
one or the other
either, never both—

There is no nuance in the light of day.
Welcome to the dark.

A LETTER TO MYSELF

No one ever told me healing hurt this much
or if they did,
my heart wasn't ready to understand:

Healing isn't the gradual and effortless
knitting together of new skin over open wounds

It's uncovering a part of your body to realise
that instead of smooth scar tissue,
there's a wound plugged only with dirt and grit and
  stubbornness
and the skin around it is inflamed
and that's why you've been aching
aching
aching

Healing is the unstoppering of wounds with foreign
  bodies
A splinter lodged in your palm that only you can
  remove
with a sterilised needled gifted to you by a therapist
or a TikTok
or a friend who went through something similar
  once.

Healing is the placing of a magnifying glass over your
   soul,
so that you can clearly see the inner structures
of a part of your insides
you never thought would be exposed
to discern which bits are you
and which bits are part of the fabric you were wearing
   when you fell
And sometimes, you get seasick trying to tell the
   difference
and so does the nurse assigned to help you.

Healing is plucking gravel, one laborious stone at a
   time, from your
knee, where you slipped thinking all was well,
when really the footwear you placed your trust in was
   slick and slippery as sin
And just as charming
And just as impractical for keeping your footing on a
   slick and slippery slope.

Healing hurts far worse
than the numbness that lies beyond exhaustion,
the brain fogog-og—ogog of burnout
when you only realise some years later
that you didn't just burn your candle at both ends,
you burned it in the middle too, then set fire to the
   stick

until the whole thing went up in a blaze, engraved
  with concepts
—like friends
—like family
—like peace
until one day,
the flame burned
out.

Healing is the long, arduous slog up a slope you ran
  quite quickly down,
led by others who ran before you who never knew,
had never been taught,
that the quickest way to the river that quenches
  thirst
just beyond the jagged, craggy hills
isn't to barrel down the slope headlong
until you roll, crashing with broken limbs, into the
  gully,
and then to *haul* yourself back up the other side,
but rather to zipline across the gully in the first place
using the wire the clever ones who came before you
  strung.

But you didn't know that
And neither did your role models
And so into the gully you ran.
Healing is a journey, fraught with tears and tempers
  and frustrations;

But, my love—
It took you years to get here.
Why do you keep assuming
it'll take only weeks to get out?
What a good thing I packed you some water
and a rainbow
and a tiny, happy potato the internet once made.

AND IN YOUR CERTAINTY, I AM MADE CERTAIN (LOVE IS REAL)

For COJL

You are so sure—
you are so sure.
Once, I worried
you'd be prepared
to fragment yourself,
a serviceable tea towel worn thin
once violet, now grey
defined by threadbare patches used
to prove your worth;
I should have read your blessing with more
faith.
But this, too, is life,
that we grow in our understanding
of prophecy as we live it.

It's not
that I wish I were as sure as you;
I know the bedrock upon which I stand.

But your surety brings me pride.
Satisfaction, in a job well done.
You are, as ever, the mountain of my heart,
guiding me home to myself.

I love you.

IN CONVERSATION WE ARE HEALED

How did I lose
touch,
my heart,
with peace
so badly that I
forget
how to breathe
and become still?

How do I
remember
my name, when my
mind is full of fog
so thick the streetlamps disappear?
I will need it again some day.

Where do I
go
to recover
me with silken

delights that bring joy
to my soul and remind me
of who I could be?

I do not need a
solution
to dissolve away my
frustration;
I ask nothing of you.
All I need
is a place
to express it
at life, the universe, and everything.

And in that place, those first
lines of superficiality disappear
and I am left with the dawn.

go
to recover
me with silken
delights that bring joy
to my soul and remind me
of who I could be;

remember

my name when my
mind is full of fog
so thick the streetlamps disappear—
I will need it again some day;

touch
my heart
with peace,
so badly that I
forget
how to breathe,
and become still.

And in that place
I ask nothing of you
and realise everything of myself;
I am the one to go, to remember
and to touch.

ABOUT WHICH I WOULD NEVER DARE

There are things
about which I
would never dare
to write a poem.

Some are too large,
great fractalling cosmoses of
thought and chaos,
light and energy sparking from one another
across the void,
an interaction
so bright no words can
contain it.

Some are too small
a microscopic moment of life
the fleeting wingbeat of a
surpassing idea;
no hummingbird here, persuadable

to drink, no matter how sweet
the water I lay out for it,
but rather a microscopic owl
a swift, silent hunter
in need of no one
and nowhere to land.

Some too painful.
Not for me—
Lord knows I've laid
my own soul bare often
enough that I've
little shame left;
but my life is never solely
my own—
Words echo on the page long
after the resonance of sound
has faded.

Some, also, too joyful:
rubbing shoulders with 'too large',
a joy so rich and infinite
long, like a golden autumn afternoon,
rich, like the wealth of the golden glowing mines,
thick and sweet like purest honey sucked
from sweetest of flowers,
light, a red leaf dancing in the breeze,
quicksilver, silver-tongued, golden-laughed,
golden, glimmering, glorious.

There are things about which I do not write
and things about which I cannot
and the world may never know the difference.

A TEACHER'S WINTER

The leaves have
gone,
blown from my branches like
your presence in my life and
I am left bare,
and bereft.

Bark cracks in the cold ice of winter,
hands and heart frozen both;
I cannot remember the sound
of your voice.
It took five weeks.
(There is something about
that number, I suspect.)

Winter may be frigid,
the ground too frozen for
new roots to take hold,
but there is value in
purging out the old;
only the strongest will
endure this season,
to rise again in the summer.

To sleep is not to dream, in this

period of cold loneliness,
or if it is it's nightmares,
where your face betrays me every time,
where I am where I'll never be again,
where emptiness is written on every line
of my body, a hollow
cocoon wherein it seems that nothing sleeps.

This is, of course, a lie.

The sharp winter frost scents the
morning air and
clear crystal skies sketch a
canopy overhead, a
glass ceiling waiting to be
shattered by the oncoming warmth
of spring, when I shall, once again,
know myself.

Ice crystals of transformative beauty and
soul-deep silences of snow and
wind chill enough to strip the pretence from your
bones and
force you to grapple with
all that's left behind...

Winter is essentialist.
It's painful, but not—you know—
bad.

AN UPDATE AT AGE TEN

My source of pride,
my fellow weirdo,
thin-skinned justice easily bruised and
determination that the world should be
fair.

How I long to scoop together all the varied pieces of
  your
bleeding heart, hold
them together as a shield
against the world which one day
will try to break you with
injustice and
unfairness and
inequity
And I do not know how to watch that day come
  about.

Sensitive and stubborn, visionary and
narrowly defined:
My big-thinker, large-picture,
spend-ten-hours-building-Lego-with-ya
engineer—

who I think,
if he can,
will engineer away all the problems of the world.

I love that you love to cook.
You made your bed this morning, the
first time in a decade,
which is horrifyingly how long you've
been alive.
What ever did I do to deserve you?

You've pushed me to my limits, grown
my patience, stretched
my knowledge, tested my
empathy and understanding and
I am so much the better for having had you in my
  life.

Truly, you are the iron that sharpens iron.

Never be afraid of the people you will impale
as you go about in this world being you.
Iron should never bend for plastic, or for wood.
Some people just weren't made
to live near greatness.

FOR THE MASTER ENABLER, AUNTY

For Clare

I don't know.
Is it a little
—cringe—
to write a poem for a friend?
It that still a thing we
—do—
these days?
Either way it's risky; poetry's
neither a mirror, nor
a lens.
Rather, it's a laser, and the
ordeal of being known
can be mortifying indeed.

But today, let us choose bravery,
and march onward in that terrifying
ordeal—sometimes known as friendship—
and let me first begin with thanks
(though no number of finite words
could ever be enough).

Thanks for always reading.
For always encouraging.
Your Huffle to my Slyther,
enabler to my goals,
one-woman personal-sized cheer squad all
wrapped up in an optimism born
of truth;
your eyes see clearly, and they choose goodness
still.

At four in the morning, I hope you remember
that.
That your presence here has sometimes been
a dawning;
that your commitment to create is like a
honeybee, ceaselessly enduring in your
fabrication of delight,
never for a moment
entertaining other ways; for you,
to create is to breathe.

(Which is not to say all breaths come
easily, I know.)

Dog sketches, dragon paintings,
'The great thing is if you hate it
you just paint right over it'.

You teach me so much about being fearless.
At four in the morning, I hope
you know that.

Poems are too liminal, words are too
ephemeral,
and there is always the matter of taste:
did any artist ever truly grasp in hand
the beauteous visions of their mind?
If they did, I am yet to behold it, but surely
it's the struggle for alignment that
mothers art into being in the first place.
That, and you.

Well, perhaps you are not *mother* to my art,
but you are more than an enabler.
…I know.
Shall we call you aunty?
Why, yes.
I think we shall.
I think my books and words and lines and poems
shall look to you collectively, all with the word
  'aunty'
dripping honey-sweet from their lips,
fondness and familiarity in their gaze,
and love, and honour, and recognition.

Thank you, then, sister, for holding my hand while I
labour these scrivenings into being;

I shall try very hard not to crush your hand with
  mine,
and shall look forward to nursing your own children
  up on my knee
in turn.

And in the meantime, I shall delight
as others do
in the golden-gleamed glow
of your art-making.

NOW OUR OWN

For Rachel

You fill my heart with
golden glimmers, glittering
rays of sunshine-coloured hope,
buoyant with helium-scented delight
for a mutual understanding
of the way the universe
is.

We are so much alike.

Talk of healing and freedom,
life and its seasons,
leaving and finding and
longing, unwinding
all the long threads of our past
to unravel
who we have become;
perhaps now we see the threads,
we can weave something even better.

You fill my heart with
silver-surfaced, shimmering, shining
waves of beach-tasting hope,

the salty promise hanging in the air
of something more
something brighter
something bespoke.

One day, both our stars will rise,
and heaven knows that so far,
based on what we have seen,
they will rise together.

Truly, you are the tide that lifts my boat.

We talk of yearning and discovering,
travel and unloving
the things we once thought integral
to our survival, and
identity.
We've both become something new
this year;
change becomes us both.

Change becomes us both, new
ballgowns of sapphired kingfisher
blue, diamond-bright tiaras upon
our heads as we
step into our mutual reign as
queens
of our own lives.

The universe will bow before us.
  Not because we overpower it.

  The universe will bow before us;
she loves to acknowledge
those who acknowledge truth.
(About the world, about connections—
about themselves. And the truth is,
we were made for more.)

You fill my heart with
pure-processed perfectly precious
platinum-patina'd peace: I
see you in the mirror, your
journey reflecting mine; it's
so much easier
to spot courage there
and divine how this story
ends.
Gratefully
I accept the reflection,
pin it to my lapel with pride.
Perhaps together, we will pull through.
Lord knows our hands now hold
enough pearls
to make anybody rich.

And anyway,
at least our lives and what we hold are now our own.

WITHOUT FIRST HAVING UN––

For Leiah, with thanks

You can only wear
one suit of clothing
at a time.

For a while, I wore
a tartan one, plaid
kneed and crisp
bloused, turned-over
snow-white socks and black
leather lace-ups, proudly lathered
to a shine.

I speak in metaphors,
and I do not.

Many have worn such
and—probably—
cast theirs away quite
easily, when the time came,
dresses shredded for catharsis or

graffitied with the sharpied love
of a thousand fickle friendships or
simply folded, one
last time, and put away,
only needed in the future as a relic,
an amusement for one's children,
a comparison such as might be made:
Oh yes, I looked like you, except
I had darker hair.
I am sure
someone somewhere
held onto theirs as long as I—
longer, even, perhaps.

Regardless, it would have been nice to know
that everyone only changes clothes
first by stripping bare.

And I don't know:
Is this something long done by
everyone who'd already laid
their uniforms to rest
and I am simply late to the party of adulthood?
Or does this come with age regardless?
Or is it both?
I'm too old for clothes no longer fit
for purpose, or for comfort
(a pandemic taught me that).

But I didn't realise
until you showed me
that I was trying to get redressed
without first having
un—.

OVER THE IDENTI-SEA

Did I read something recently
about another culture
wherein it is said that
other people know you
better than yourself?
Adrift, unmoored, having let
my dock lines go,
I well believe this to be true.

When I cut anchor to allow
myself to be blown out
across the sea uncharted
(not in its entirety, but
at least by me),
I knew something of the
seasickness
I'd face. It's difficult
to care who you are
when you're puking out your guts.
Maslow (and I assume the guy he stole it from)
would heartily approve.

But the boat isn't sailing any more,
or if it is, it's daring little hops up

and down the coast, skipping like a stone from
island to island under the bright
golden sun,
and sometimes the sun is blistering,
and sometimes the sun is hiding,
but it's nothing to the mast-high
gunwale-breeching
wave-crashing
soul-destroying
ship-wrecking seas
I've crossed of late.

On this side of calm, I'm not
sure what I look like anymore.
Like I left every silvered mirror that I owned
back
on the other side of a teal-green ocean of
chasmic-dark waves,
and now the only way to see
who I am
is to be reliant
on those around me: my new school
of silvered, mirrored fish,
jewels hanging in
subtropical waters I
now call home.

They are too generous by halves.
Of course, I love them for it.

FOR MY AUDIENCE OF ONE

AL: i need to keep reminding myself that poetry is
writing too

LB: it is
so is texting me

AL: lol
i'm not sure i can quite convince myself of that
in terms of the "by writing we here mean 'create
something new and beautiful in the world'" but
otoh why the heck not i guess
so sure
okay
typing to you counts
this is an act of creation
and beauty
a poem
for my audience
of one.

A HOUSE BY DAY / BY DARK

The tiny house
where once I lived
looms large in
lingering dreams.

By day
the townhouse is neutral:
slightly apricot walls
slightly grey carpet
(I think? Or was it beige?)
slightly small
slightly homey slightly fraying slightly
bare.
Immaculately clean, at
least at first,
but still too small or else why
would the baby be sleeping
in the lounge room?

I remember fish leaping from
their bowls for three months straight,
a run of suspicious baby koi longing

for freedom or
curiosity or
air.

I remember the dark wood dining
table, set with cream candles, sweet flowers,
ferny greenery and fragile finery on a
Friday evening, or else huddled round
with foil-enveloped faces, steaming
away the impurities from our skin
as though it could steam them away
from our hearts as well.
For a little while, it did.

An arctic display of toys, a sofa bed for sleep
overs, a black trampoline used more often
as a tent, and a tent yellowing the grass
every summer for months on end, until
only the square silhouette of its
footprint remained to be sprinklered away
when school returned.
Digging for quartz pebbles in the mulch until
it too was grassed over; pink primroses and
yellow Banksia roses and burgundy-red Japanese
maple leaves and blue-and-pink hydrangeas
holding glistening-wrapped birthday-
present books like petalled chests full
of secret treasure.

I remember my sister's bush-themed
birthday, pin-the-redback-on-the-web,
three bears picnicking on a chocolate cake log,
a bonbon made of tissue paper, filled
with a white velvety unicorn and far
far far too much glitter.
It got everywhere, lingering for years.
Funny how some things do that.

There was a witch, too, marred by the stars
that glowed softly from my bookcase,
a face made from shadows and imagination,
a cackling made from fear and shame.

The grey rabbit lived in my atrium for a while,
a secret little garden of pots and snails that
crunched under my bare heels one night
when I walked out there unprepared.
It was a high-walled, fully-enclosed space,
with garden shade cloth over top
(peach, apricot, beige, some nondescript
neutral like that); where
on *earth* did the snails come from?

At night,
the townhouse is often twice its
size, recognisable only
upon waking.
In the manner of dreams, doors

distort; windows yawn with
hungry maws, or else eyes
too large for comfort.
It seems I'm always running
in these dreams,
though they start
innocuously enough.

From the outside, proportions
skew into discomfort, and
from the inside, the windows are
too wide, too high, too open
to the dark, gleaming sky outside, where
someone is always
watching
from the stars, or the
shadows, like a
witch's face cackling
in the night.

A large dog, chasing me down with
teeth too long and sharp;
me, huddling behind the curtains in
the front, the formal lounge
(where the baby slept, where I
rocked her for hours on end
when all she wanted was her
mother, who I was
not), with someone, indefinable in

the manner of dreams, lurking,
leering, lingering outside the house's
front door, which is suddenly
open, only an insecure screen, an easily
torn veil, separating
me from whatever horror
lay hidden yet beyond.

The garage, built for a dual-car family,
suddenly cavernous and warehouse-huge,
a maze of steel chains and beige roller doors to
navigate
hurriedly before whoever owns
the place comes back to where
oil stains mar the
concrete floor and
shadows flicker in dim light.

A walk under casuarina pines along a
concrete footpath, innocuous enough, until
I lose my way and the sky grows grey and
suddenly I'm running, running, though
I'm not sure why and
on the horizon
the house,
over-large, over-distant, unreachable until
suddenly I do and it's no good because
the reason I'm running has circum-
navigated the park and beat me home

and it's there, and it's dark, and it's
inside.

The house was sealed with happy
memories, or so I thought; how
did the horrors get inside?
My childhood was sealed with
joy and love, or so
I thought; how did the horrors
get outside?

EMERALD ENOUGH TO EAT

When a horse has run full
sprint, for mile
after mile
after mile,
sides lathered with sweat whipped
into white foam like waves
on the waning seas,
flanks heaving, earthquake-trembling,
heavy, laborious, cumbersome,
head drooping to the ground,
sagging like a puppet deprived both
of volition and desire…
we do not ask it to continue sprinting.

When a horse is pushed too far,
sometimes, it breaks a
leg. And then,
there is nothing left to do
but put it down.

I feel put down.

Society demands I run,
mile after
mile after
mile, when
my flanks are heaving,
my sides are lathered with foam,
and I am broken, not in leg per se
but in spirit.
My head, too, is sagging.

The apparent solution is pasture,
but even that
has negative connotations.
No one *wants*
to be put out to pasture, even if
the grass is greener.
Emeralds are all well
and good, but you
can't eat them to survive,
no matter how starved a horse
you are.

But still, you rest
or you break.
Society may reject you for it, but
the grass will welcome you home.

HEAR ME OUT

WHAT IF—
and hear me out here,
just for a moment—
there's nothing actually
WRONG
with you.

You
are not a problem
to be solved,
a puzzle to
be completed,
a riddle in need
of rhyme.

There are
no answers
or if there are
they don't matter
one jot.
You think
they'll help.
They won't.

So you look at the world
sideways.
So your life looks different
to others.
And?

No but seriously:
and??

Different is not a puzzle
either,
though God knows
we make it one.

WHAT IF—
hear me out—
you are
perfect
designed
impassioned and
lovely,
a you that only you
could conceive.

I'm not talking about
your brokenness,
not seeking to invalidate
any healing you desire;

but think
upon all the ways
society has trained you to think
that you are less
when really
society was the one seeking
to do less
for you.

A raven's only black
in a crowd of doves.

Subway stations and dusky wings,
wheelchair ramps and a heart that sings
pills and alarms,
apps for mind-calm…
Perhaps you simply
weren't meant
for a 9 to 5,
wilderness soul fighting
to survive,
corporate jungle world
hell-bent
on caging you to
change your spots and
grind you down, daily
sieve idiosyncrasities
from your soul
until you emerge—

dutiful little factory worker,
marching time with
all the other dutiful
little factory workers.

WHAT IF—
hear me out here—
you're not a problem
in need
of solving

and you never
were?

MAKE HER OWN

A girl picked up
a four-leafed clover
spotted by chance
a wayside encounter
on a path
leading elsewhere
than home.

As she walked, she held it,
pressed between forefinger and thumb
as though they were the pages
of a Bible
filled with a wisdom of their own.

Then, stooping,
she laid the four-leaf clover,
pressed flat, upon the asphalt
for some other traveller to find
and the breeze picked up
and the clover blew away into the wind
swirling upwards to infinity…

…and so, stooping,
she laid the four-leaf clover,
pressed flat, upon the asphalt
for some other traveller to find,
and the next person walking
down the path the girl had trod
found it there and discarded it with a glance,
crushing the clover to rags
beneath their boot…

…and so, stooping,
she laid the four-leaf clover,
pressed flat, upon the asphalt
for some other traveller to find
and a child spied it and became
like a red balloon rising
against dark and fulsome rain clouds

And a young man saw it and smiled
And an old woman saw it and smiled
And they saw it too and smiled

and even if the clover spiralled
off into the wind,
fractalling on storm-scented air
lit up by the glowing, gilding
light of evening sun beneath the
clouds, unseen;

even if the girl forgot
the day she chanced
tangible luck on the wayside
on the long road
home, or somewhere
else entirely…

It didn't matter
and it did—
either way, she'd let it go.
She'd make her own.

AN ENTREPRENEURIAL
SPRING

When one thinks of spring, ordinarily
what comes to mind may be
bees, or
flowers, bulbs or
buds, brisk breezes and
warming sunshine, emerald
grass and—excuse me—
urine-scented blossoms.
(Have you ever *smelled*
an ornamental pear tree?)

Hayfever, too, that itchy, sneezing
curse that signals change;
or layers, the donning, the shedding;
a gradual emerging
from the den of winter,
the person we used to be,
a blinking in bright light, a
false awakening before a sudden
freeze (Oh no! Surely winter's
gone this time?) and then the gradual
thawing (it prickles) into growth (a painful stretching).

Once, I was something else. (A seed, a seedling,
    almost withered.)
I'm thawing now. (Some leaves were burnt; enough
    survive.)

When one thinks of spring, its
actual
focus rarely springs to mind:
This season's all about the pollen.
More, this season's all about the
    —*CROSS POLLI NATION*—.
The mixing of ideas, abstractions,
the blending of concepts, refraction,
the merging together of bitter-
tasting products, which,
mixed amply with some bee-spit
(like elbow-grease, one imagines),
create a kind of sweetness
lacking anywhere else
in nature.

Emerging into the light, I see
for the first time
the sweetness of what might be,
and at last the weather's warm enough
to cross-pollinate
ideas until they
become both fertile, blossoms
fading into branches laden with produce,

and also honey, a sweet glaze
transmogrified
from the bitter
sneeze-bringing
detritus
of my past life.

I used to think I was an autumn girl.
Perhaps I always will be,
but this year,
I'm learning to enjoy
the spring—
in my step, in my heart,
all around.
And for once,
I'm eager
for the fruit
that maybe this time
I won't be required
to fall from.

This bee's awoken.
Let the pollination begin.

ENOUGH FOR DAILY WEAR

Quick to love and
slow to trust:
that's me,
and what I'm slow to trust is this:
that my regular self is perfectly
good enough
for daily wear, and that for
others, wearing it so
will not wear it thin.

I realise now that
this second-guessing
micro-reading
triple-checking insecurity
was a lesson never meant
for me.
That was someone else's
curriculum, and they
weren't supposed to pass it on.

There is nothing wrong
with me, and
one day, daily,
I will wear that.

UNMAZED

I dreamed of you again last night, and
you turned your face away from me and
ignored me.

I was there to help you, support you, ensure
you had everything you needed to succeed
as you waited there in the cavernous hall
for your examinations to begin.
I took the papers you needed copied and
unmazed my way to the library where
stacks had grown storeys high and
photocopiers perched like peregrine
falcons, out of reach, almost out of
sight, in dim, foggy, spectral rafters never made
for such machines.

I found one, finally, a scanner I could reach,
and its insides lay open and exposed, no
glass screen to shield them from dust and damage,
or to facilitate the copying I'd
brought with me for you,

and anyway, the pages had now changed and
I realised copying them wouldn't help you,
for these weren't the papers that you needed
after all.

I left.

I've no idea if you succeeded.

UNTETHERED AND REFEATHERED

I am untethered, as I
have said before, but
this time, in this season,
what I am untethered from,
is the granitine weight
of expectation.

To live free from self-judgement
is a heady flight and
this bird soars.

I never realised the cage I
was in until after
the lock had been picked and
I was out, hopping awkwardly on
the concrete with
stunted wings I hadn't known
my previous employ
had clipped.

Ten years is a long time

to blame yourself for
your inability to fly.

Four months
is a long time
to spend unpicking the
trauma of that belief (and
nowhere near enough).

Birds might fledge in mere weeks,
but I will take longer to
recondition my flight muscles and
remember how to glide again
(if I ever knew).

Flight feathers itch
to regrow.
Flight muscles burn
to rebuild.
But that first heady leap
from the cliff, the spiralling
tumbling fall, and
that moment when your wings first
catch the air, sweeping
your stomach out from under you as you
realised just how close you came
to disaster

and the disaster wasn't from leaping
but rather the glaciers
encroaching at the top of the cliff
that may have crushed you there
forever,
only you leapt just in time, and you
free fell, trusting that your wings
would recondition as you plunged—
and so that moment
when you first soar
and all your risk-taking was justified...

That is the true untethering.
And now is the real re-feathering
as the clipped ones fall
away.

ALL HAIL SPRING RAIN

All hail
the season of green
growing things and green
bellied clouds carrying
marbles of ice
that smash and shatter
and shred.

Tenderly, the almost-summer sun
bathes baby beets and
silvery-stalked spinach and
fragrant orange blossoms;
I put in sweet potatoes today.
I was so proud, because
only real gardeners grow
sweet potato.

Ferociously, in a scant six
minutes of fury, late
spring hail smashed the garden flat,
and I have welts all over my

back, which prickle and tingle
like pins and needles, only instead
it was marbles of ice.
At the time, I imagined I was
paint balling,
though that didn't make
me less mad
when the hailstones hit
my skull.

I knew I'd be sore tonight, after
hours of hauling concrete to
reinforce the chicken coop where
last month, a russet-red, bushy-tailed,
demon-eyed murderbeast got in,
pursuing two poor haunted hens
around the yard until red ran over
the clover-studded lawn—
blood and feathers both.
Twenty bags of twenty kilos each of
silver-grey powder-fine cement
should prevent this tragedy reoccurring,
though the newly laid concrete
was nearly a tragedy itself
when the hail came down—
saved by a sky blue tarp,
much like our car was saved by
a quick-thinking bit of chipboard and
some rolls of roofing insulation—

excellent cushioning for the car,
less so for the humans holding it
in place,
and now my knuckles are blushing
purple and red and my feet
that were bare are welted and blanched
and my back looks much like my
imaginings of paintball were correct.
I knew I'd be sore tonight; I didn't
imagine it would be from doing battle
with a storm.

And to think, this morning I wished
that it would rain.

IN WHICH SPRING DEMONSTRATES NEATLY TWO WAYS OF CHANGE IN A SINGLE DAY

Firstly, the slow and gradual unbudding
of a tiny, tiny seed, a lettuce that took
so long to come up we'd given up
hope and tried again, Australian yellow
leaf sown right over the Tennis Ball—
or was it Lakes Great? Whichever one
it was, it took its time. Days and days,
some so cold it seemed that it might
snow in fluffy, frozen flakes the week
right before summer was due, some so
sweltering you felt your cheeks burn
lobster just contemplating time spent out-of-shade.
The other seeds came up, the other lettuce—
Tennis Ball? Lakes Great? Whichever one
it was, it was faster, that was sure—
and the carrots were all up now too,
purple dragons and something vibrantly orange

and maybe some white and yellow in there too;
the beets were making a second appearance,
due to be sliced open to reveal their concentric
target-ring centres of white and burgundy and
burgundy and white several months' hence
from now. The beans had popped up almost
right away, bursting through damp soil and
sweet-smelling straw-coloured mulch barely
a week after they'd been lovingly cocooned
in the earth—eager, as always, to get started.

But the lettuces? The slow ones?
They came through today, growing in
their own time, at their own pace, when
conditions were right for what they needed,
and not a minute before.

Secondly, the darkening of the sky, followed
closely by cracks of thunder too high and loud
for cannons, illuminated by flashes like
the sky was trying to take our photograph;
we flinched, and scanned the sky for the deep
green belly of the cloud that signals ice.
We heard it, though, before we saw it, a scant
two-minute warning that starts a scant
two minutes after the thunder: a roar, like
a never-ending ocean wave or the wind
raging through a forest or—in actual fact—
like hail, the size of glass children's marbles

and just as solid, pelting from the sky like it
was trying to win at paintball. The speedboat storm
sprinted past, not even breaking double digits
in its visit, but breaking in its wake all our
dreams and expectations. Potatoes, snapped
and shredded. The plum tree, naked. Fig
leaves torn like sails salvaged from a shipwreck.
Sweet potatoes decimated and seedlings crushed...
—This is the second type of change.

Of course, it doesn't have to be this way; slow
change can cause destruction too, and fast isn't
always bad. It might be interesting to note,
  however,
that because the lettuces were so tiny,
they endured the hail without harm.

MY HUSBAND'S DESK

There is a bag of rolled oats on
the printer and if that
isn't a microcosm of our
lives right now, I don't know
what is.
Vibrant orange, same shade
as the fruit, conjuring dripping
juices and oil-rich peel and
sticky, acid-sweet segments—
which is, let's face it, nothing
like the contents of the packet,
which are currently dry, flat grains,
slightly powdery, a little sweet-
smelling to be sure, and gloopy
when soaking wet, which is why—
to be honest—we bought them—
where was I going?

This, too, is a microcosm of
our lives.

The desk is strewn with maps and
plans, geometric angles on geometrically
folded paper, annotations delineating
rooms in measurements red, and green—
like Christmas, except not on the tree,
because our tree—ten foot tall with
glittering, glistening fingers and
gleaming, golden globes and shimming
silver spheres and birds the colour of
furry-soft sage, or olive leaf, some even
aqua or teal—our tree is a
compromise of colours, neither
gold-and-red, nor
silver-and-blue—
but the plans are still annotated in red and in green
and
that is a hint at the promise contained within,
at least for the ones who've commissioned them.

This is, if not my life, then his.

I should explain the oats. They're for
a camp. Not for eating, but for soaking
overnight and then for throwing.
Deliberately.
Delightedly.
At each other.
The camp is for children, and we are
the visionary staff.

Another synecdoche.

Post-it notes and highlighters—his—
a mug of raspberry black tea—mine—
two giant screens small countries away—
his, and I am envious; my work screens
are much much closer and my eyes are
mimicking the distance, my vision
growing shorter like the weeks
left in the year.

I see he has my password there, under
a screen, a curled yellow post-it like
a daisy pressed for preservation,
a moment captured in time with value
beyond its physicality; this password is
the access to my laptop, which is to say
my brain.

A jar of pens that once held jam, and—
if we could ever find a lid to match—
might one day hold jam again.

Another microcosm.

Rulers and document racks, pencils and
staplers, spiral-bound notebooks and black
lever folders in quirky rows with white labels,
three of them, like the family of magpies that

have adopted our yard. The car keys, his wallet,
the teal desk chair where I can't touch the floor
(still more comfortable than mine), a bright
orange USB nearly matching the mandarin
shine of the oat bag; samples of varied upholstery
destined for our bus camper (though where *it*
is destined, nobody knows; a project much greater
in scope and in time than we ever imagined—
how appropriate).

And then there's me, appropriating the desk
that isn't mine, with my tea and my MacBook
and my one foot dangling from an old padded chair
that came with the house when we moved.
What ideas are created here, at this desk, which is
such a universe, uniquely its own and yet so
reflective of the wider world beyond,
less so a desk and more so a mirror, cluttered
with the mirroring of us.

PIER SPACINGS FOR ONE-WAY SPANNING WALLS

I don't know what it means
to one-way span a wall, despite the table
on the wall of my husband's office
purporting to enlighten me;
I do understand the concept of
spacing out one's piers, though.
And I imagine, that much like
a one-way spanning wall,
there ought to be similar rules
for how regularly one's personal
support piers
ought to be spaced.

Half-hourly: as often, I think,
as I ought to space out my
eye-break-spanning piers.
At least hourly: as often, I expect,
as I ought to space out my
get-up-and-walk-around support piers.

What about the cry-out-my-emotions piers?
What's the appropriate interval for that?
Or my gather-and-debrief-with friends?
What about my take-a-day-off-for-no-reason-
other-than-that-you-wanted-one piers?
My hug-my-children-while-they're-little?
My close-the-laptop-and-go-to-bed support piers?
My eat-less-sugar-so-I-actually-sleep-at-night?

I expect some of this depends on the width
of the pier. What is the load-bearing capacity
of a ten-minute hug with my husband?
Of a half-hour session of quiet reading?
Of a page and a half of journalling in
rainbow-coloured pens? (I do expect the rainbows
add at least a little to its capacity.)

And where is the rule book for tea and
hot baths? For saying no to hustle or
volunteering at church? How often should
I be out in my garden, and when should
I skip making a tasty vegetable dinner
in favour of an earlier bedtime for the children?
(A support pier of mine as much as it is of
theirs.)

Ah, the table also says it depends on the
height of the wall, and the class of the wind.

On a fair day, with a low wall, one imagines
the support piers can be quite flimsy, really,
and still fulfil their intended purpose just fine.
In a hailstorm, with a wall that weighs
as much as the world on your shoulders,
I imagine the support piers ought to be sturdier.

Probably, I should internalise that, and stop
chastising myself for needing stronger piers
when perhaps what I need
is to step out of the wind,
and put down the wall that is, if I do,
unnecessarily high.
One needn't construct a mountain,
after all, simply to keep out a mole.

OLD STORIES NEW

I think it's been three years
since I was walking into work on
a dewy early morning after rain,
the pristine lawn still bathing,
immaculate sidewalks towelling
themselves down under sauna steam
in the hot early sunshine, the sky
new-washed and wrinkled but
dry.

On the concrete, a worm lay dying,
not an inch from ground that was
no longer sodden and inhospitable.

Benevolently, I applied a gentle fingertip.
Spasming, the worm protested.

My touch was unfamiliar enough that
having its life saved was unpleasant.
For three years, I thought that was the moral:
The struggle against assistance, the fight
against the change.

Now what stands out to me is this:
The inch-wide gap between the worm and
safety; a distance half the length of Worm
from a place that once held danger—
drowning, suffocation, drenched in a
downpour that forced the worm to flee—
but which was now the only hope for refuge.
It wasn't stubbornness
that occasioned the worm to flinch
from a finger coaxing it to safety.
Rather, in the baking sun,
like an old story the concrete had outlived
its usefulness as a life preserver.
Like a poem that goes on too long—

A REPRIORITISED SUMMER

Being patient
is the itchiest feeling in the world.
You oughtn't scratch
—you really, really oughtn't—
but the scratching is nonetheless
inevitable.

You pick at the surface:
What am I waiting for?
Have I finished healing yet?
Can I take this cast off?
Can I *run*?

But when you're really, truly
broken,
then no:
You cannot.

The itch starts as a general
kind of restlessness, a
dissatisfaction with your
productivity levels or

how you spent your day—
a feeling you're well used to,
if you're honest, though
you're used to it coming
from a different source.

It spreads into your soul next,
a miasma of desperate hope
lessness, welling up like an odorous
balloon in your gut, which you
try to deflate, to ignore.

But then impatience breaches
the blood-brain barrier
and the itch infects
your mind.
It's almost the constant rumbling
mutterings of the lion called anxiety,
but if you pick at it around the edges,
the itch is deeper,
outlined by a sense of dread.
You've never felt this panicked
in your life.

What if you really are broken?
What if the healing never comes?
You stare desperately at other runners

passing you by and wonder
if the cast was really worth it, or if
you could maybe have kept on running
on a broken leg after all.

Being patient is the itchiest feeling
of all, all consuming, all encompassing,
and you know—you *know*—
the solution is just to *be* patient
but simple was never
a synonym for easy.

And yet, somehow, you know:
this is all part of the free fall,
the trusting, the letting go;
this *is* the faith-leap: that some day
you will get better (you believe),
that stopping to rest will see you
run faster in the long run (you assume),
that reprioritising your entire life
to accommodate tiredness that never seems to
diminish, that instead seems, like an onion, to
grow more layers the more you
peel them back—the Onion of Tiredness,
the Infinite Parfait of Exhaustion—
you've reprioritised your life around
them, and now...

Well.

Now is the baking summer that seeks to see
whether your faith will flourish or wither.
And Heaven knows you
don't want to be
one of those people
who give up
right before it gets
easy.

THE CALM IN BETWEEN

The moment
of the dive is
not silent; a shivering
splash,
the thunder of bubbles—
but the next moment
as you glide, graceful, gull-like,
a sleek seal streaming effortless
through water aquamarine
and blue

at the bottom, for just
a moment,
the momentum holds
you down
and you glance up to the sunlight
up above:
golden glimmers slice the ripples
shimmering, shifting, shaping
a fractalled, underwater world
of possibilities too numerous
to understand.

There is a moment,
before your breath begins to burn
aching for air,
before your eyes blur from
sharp chlorine chemicals,
before buoyancy bears you back
to the surface where wind
will break over you, bringing
chills and goosebumps of
reality…

In that liminal moment,
between dive and
resurface,
there is only

you

languid
liquid
alive.

A SUMMER SUNSET STORM

It was the sunset
that flipped the switch:
And I should have known,
because at the end of every truly hot day
there comes a storm,
ominous and anvil-headed, blue-grey
belly pregnant with pure, unbridled bolts
of energy—untameable, unstoppable, and
awesome.
Of course, even the most avid storm-lover
jumps
when a really big booming cracker goes
off right over your head.

The sunset lured me with cotton-candy
hues and glowing golden rays, attention-
grabbing, breath-taking, awe-inspiring,
muse-worthy.
How fortunate we are
to have innate a sense of beauty,
which is—fundamentally—superfluous for survival.
(It didn't have to be this way.)

And like that, the dam was breached,
the storm gates opened, thunderous
torrential rain flooded down
and in this vast and gushing flow,
oceanic, tidal, monsoonal,
I danced, arms up-stretched, face up-
turned, soul a-glow as the pelting,
drenching, quenching, roaring rain
filled me up inside.

Rainwater flowed like ink through my veins.
The words returned.
The drought was at an end.

BUTTERFLY-FEST

The butterflies are not
the reason I am here, but
they would be reason enough:
a thousand of them or more,
borne in on the breast of a storm
front that rumbles blue-grey in the distance
like a promise, but which, having
skirted the distance around our
grassy flat on the top of a hill within
spitting distance of the tallest one in Australia,
vanishes again without a trace
of rain, instead leaving flurries of
white butterflies to thicken
in its wake.

I lie in grass the colour of the dried
hay it is, pale gold, sweet scented,
intimate and familiar like a horse's breath,
physically in the tent where I am supposed
to be meeting but mentally
outside, and I have cunningly angled

myself so I can see the sky above;
a clear sky is deep, but a cerulean one
bedecked with horse-tail cirrus that whirlpool
slowly across its depths is infinite.

The butterflies wing from every direction, not
congested but constant, heavy air traffic if they
were the kind with two wings and an engine,
traversing across the zenith like satellites, too
  distant to
see their wingbeats, so far I am honestly surprised
I can see them at all, some mere white specks
against the paisley of sky and cloud,
cloud and sky.

Occasionally, two or three meet in spiralling
whirling dances—spin, twist, glide—before
parting ways once again, and the sky is littered
with sonder; how *does* it feel to be a butterfly?
I do not know, but I am blessed by their passing
regardless.

CAMPOREE 2023 A

The mountaintop was smaller
this time
than last, although the grassy incline
from tent to eucalyptus-hemmed activity
site is greater this time
than my weakened hips
would have liked.

I came seeking songful immersion,
waves of sound and rhythm cascading over
my body, drowning anxiety away like
saltwater purifying the skin through
immersion, reaching the deepest, innermost
places of my mind and inducing
calm.

Perhaps I was too wound up,
this time.

Peace feels like a fragile, tenuous
thing and my emotions are like
spun glass or a misty cloud or cotton candy,
which I used to call fairy floss until

I spent three days spinning hours
from it and now it's all I see
in the dark behind my eyes, a backdrop
to all my running-commentary thoughts,
billowing forth from the machine
indeed like cobwebby cotton, spun.

They sung all the songs I liked and knew
the one night I elected not to go,
opting instead for an early night after
a week of hard labour and small-seeming hills;
I feel cheated of my mountain—
if God indeed wants me close to Him,
why did I miss my song service?
All I wanted was the joy I found here
last time.

I'm trying hard to see the lesson
but honestly:

I'm devastated enough to weep
into my musty pillow, alone in the
sweat-soaked dark, except that canvas walls
are far too thin and
tissues in short supply.

I didn't expect the mountaintop of
this time
to taste like disappointment.

CAMPOREE 2023 B

A short cry does wonders
for one's perspective, salt water
purging cortisol from the body, and I
recall now that
last time
my fall from the mountaintop
as I returned to reality was
as a man falls from a cliff:
a headlong plummet, wingless,
through thin air that slowly thickens
until it is suffocating and rank as the
rockface of the cliff races past until
the mountaintop is naught but a
distant memory of a time when one
remembered how to be more
than a creature lost in the darkness
of a crevasse.

This time,
the mountaintop may be smaller,
but I expect the fall will be
correlatively so.

Or perhaps, this time, I may not fall at all,
for the fall is only of the mind,
and if there is to be a lesson
this time,
it is that no prayers will erase
the needs of the body I've been given.
There are many miracles I have prayed
into being, a conduit for divinity, both
this week and in other, lower times;
but it seems now, when I am finally
starting to listen, when I am finally
starting to see how badly
I've treated my body over the years,
abuse born of insufficiency and an
inability to contemplate the
worthiness of myself in repose,
now any prayer that seeks to erase
the mundane needs of my flesh
will not be answered. Not for I
the miracle of a scalp de-itched and
de-insomnified at 3am; instead, this
transubstantiation is a frozen
shower in an icy breeze as goosebumps
prickle my skin like the persistent prayers
of the broken.

Perhaps, this time, then,
the mountaintop is not for my mind or
my soul but instead for my
body, the third figure of my personal trinity I've
sorely neglected these past seven years,
and perhaps, this time,
it is time
that we transition from the cows of famine
to the cows of plenty, in a biblical reversal of fate.
I should like to think, then, that if
last time,
the fall was in my mind, perhaps
this time
the steadiness of the terrain will remain
within my body.

CAMPOREE 2023 C

Fear is an altar
I have worshipped at too long.
Like the heat of evening that
overstays its welcome, or
the tickling scent of sweet hay
grass that seduces before
enfevering, like bread left to
bake in the heat of a canvased,
zippered tent until it dries and
turns to crumbs,
so too is the fear that has kept me
moving for so long.
Anxiety is an ever-turning wheel.
I am tired of playing the hamster.

Both frustrating and beautiful
is the way in which something familiar
hits differently when your mind
is ripe; I have seen the bees hover
around lemon flowers still tightly
closed until they abandon them for
more welcoming repositories, and it seems
my mind, although it budded, had
ne'er yet fully bloomed, for when I saw on stage
the cries of pain, the lash of whip, the

crown of thorns—clouded mirrors
though they be—it was not that they
were new to me, or I to them, but rather
that the lemon blossom of my mind
was this time open for pollination.

I never wanted someone hurt for me.
I never asked for someone to save me.
I thought I'd always been grateful, though
until this time
all I could think was, Let me take your place.
To wrestle with that is to be a
croc fighter, grappling a concept that
has teeth, and will shortly turn and bite.
I do not like to see suffering; that much
speaks well to my character.
But to refuse a gift freely given, over which I
have no say or input or control, on the
grounds that it brings me discomfort…
Discomfort is a crocodile that, when it
smiles, reveals teeth inscribed, like diamonds,
with 'debt' and 'undeserving', which rest
upon foundations themselves inscribed with 'fear'.

It is not for me to determine my worth.
It is not for me to refuse
a gift freely given.
And the truth of the matter is this:
A debt I can never repay;

the knowledge that I am deemed worthy and
repayment was never required.
This is a much loftier altar, adorned with
golden clouds and rays of light that requires
raising my eyes from my own
troubles and looking into the hazy-dawned
future, which brightens with gold-and-pastel fingers
as promises slowly bloom in the morning light.

Two years' journey has culminated in this:
the soul-deep realisation
that the foundations of my fear-strewn altar
rest upon unworthiness I have devised
in the melting magma of my own heart,
and that to shed fear is to accept
the discomfort of debt—and to grow slowly
into a yoke that is easy and a burden that is
far lighter than the cumbersome weight
of the burnt offerings and sacrifice
demanded by anxiety.

No more
will I worship
at a lion-like altar of my own
creation.

(As it transpires,
I have found my mountaintop
after all.)

CHANGE IS IN THE WIND (AND I AM SOARING)

This summer
has been unusually windy.
People say it's La Niña, but
I think it's actually a
metaphor: change is in the wind.

Oh, for sure, there will be lightning (lightening)
storms aplenty, and no doubt
winter's ice will still freeze, and leaves
will still be shed. Hail will plummet
through the air and thunder will
grumble and growl like the lion
that used to prowl within me and
who tries still to make my heart
its home; but this year,
this year,
I have learned a secret:
I know now how to fly, and it is
(with apologies) merely falling
but with style
so one doesn't hit the ground.

Flight feathers emerging, proud lion
diminishing, courage emboldening,
worthiness the bedrock upon which
I define my immortal soul,
I look this time toward autumn—in
life and metaphor both, perhaps—
with the dove of hope at home in
the great oak tree of my mind,
and I wonder if perhaps
this year,
there will be no fall.

And I wonder, what will I do
with this new-found free-soaring
heart-buoying, tide-lifting, ocean-faring,
un-mazing emerald-greening re-clothing pier-
  spanning
re-tethering new-feathering
lion-taming
freedom?

I am a butterfly, with no path left to
travel but the future.

What shall I do?

I know.
Perhaps I'll write a book.

#AUTUMN GIRL

#I'm an autumn girl #feed me the golden light that drips like honey from curling leaves #leaves that shed safety anchors to fly free on wind that could take them anywhere #syrupy afternoons long and slow like nothing matters #except savouring the waning old-summer days #pin me down with the comforting weight of four feather doonas on my bed #my limbs sinking into the cocooning mattress with all the heaviness of deep calm #feed me hot chocolate evenings and crisp apple mornings #feel the bite of winter promises in the morning air #summer mornings are blush blue #but autumn ones grow teeth #layer me up with black cardigans and magenta scarves #I'll shed them by lunch time like an old skin #brave as bees in the pumpkin-spice air #unroll me fresh potatoes from their mounds with skins gleaming yellow and purple and pink #who needs gemstones with treasures like these #it's like grow-your-own-jewellery right at home #send me the scent of early woodsmoke as the heating cranks up once again #let me soothe my soul by finding warmth when my body is cold #walk me through woods turned butternut and hazel and butter-bright and wine #I do love a city that dresses itself with the seasons #ever-changing #ever evolving #never static #always growing #there's something savouring about the change of autumn #inviting you to linger #and something savoury #delicious and sustaining #and something sweet #indulgent and rewarding #the perfect balance #the perfect blend #autumn girl #forever

ABOUT THE AUTHOR

AMY LAURENS is an Australian author of fantasy fiction for all ages. Her story *Bones Of The Sea*, about creepy carnivorous mist and bone curses, won the 2021 Aurealis Award for Best Fantasy Novella.

Amy has also written the award-winning portal-fantasy *Sanctuary* series about Edge, a 13-year-old girl forced to move to a small country town because of witness protection (the first book is *Where Shadows Rise*), the humorous fantasy *Kaditeos* series, following newly graduated Evil Overlord Mercury as she attempts to acquire a castle, the young adult series *Storm Foxes*, about love and magic and family in small town Australia, and a whole host of non-fiction.

Head to www.AmyLaurens.com to find out more!

Read more by Amy Laurens!

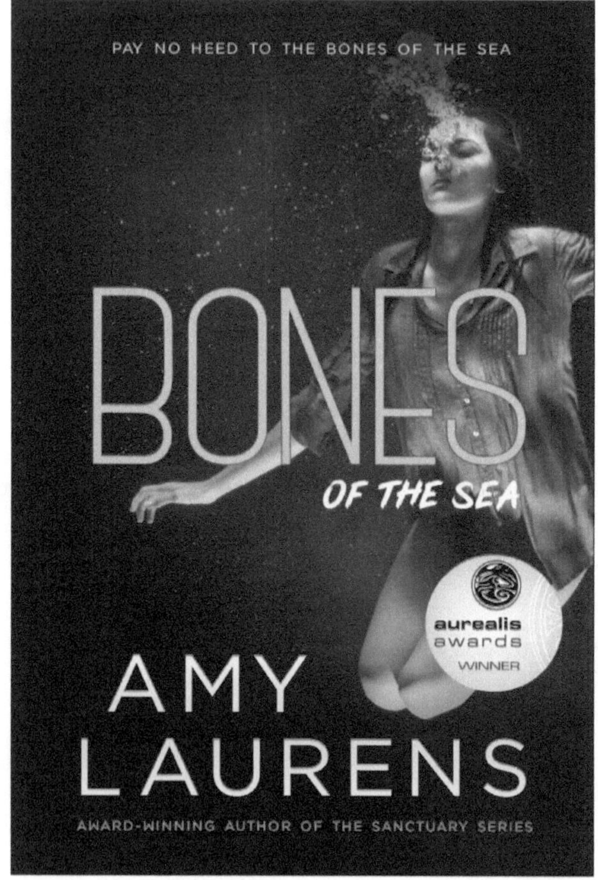

FOR A
Little While
A COLLECTION OF POEMS
AMY LAURENS

April Showers

Six rainy autumn stories

Award-winning author of the Sanctuary series

AMY LAURENS